God gives new life

A book of 30 Bible readings and notes to
help you worship and pray

This book was written by **Pearl Bridge**, **Suzy Edmundson**
and **Derek Thompson**, with a little help and encouragement
from friends. It was edited by **Tony Phelps-Jones**.

Published by Scripture Union, 207–209 Queensway, Bletchley, MK2 2EB, England.

Email: info@scriptureunion.org.uk
Internet: www.scriptureunion.org.uk

© Copyright all editions Causeway PROSPECTS
Published by Causeway PROSPECTS as God Gives New Life in 2000.

First published in this revision by Scripture Union in 2004.
ISBN 1 85999 064 5

Causeway PROSPECTS is a division of PROSPECTS for People with Learning Disabilities, and their address is PO Box 351, Reading, RG30 4XQ. Phone 0118 9516 978. Email: causeway@prospects.org.uk

About Causeway PROSPECTS: Causeway PROSPECTS provides resource materials and training to equip churches for effective outreach and ministry among people with learning disabilities. It also runs holiday weekends and special ministry at Spring Harvest and the Keswick Convention.

British Library Cataloguing-in-Publication Data: a catalogue record for this book is available from the British Library.

Scripture portions are taken from The Holy Bible: English Version for the Deaf (published as the Easy-to-Read Version) © 1995 by World Bible Translation Center, Inc. and used with permission. Internet: www.wbtc.com

Icons © Widgit Software Ltd 2002, developed by the Rebus Symbol Development Project, designed by Cate Detheridge, and used with kind permission.

Cover design by David Lund Design, Milton Keynes.

Printed and bound in Great Britain by goodmanbaylis, The Trinity Press, Worcester, UK.

≤ **Scripture Union:** We are an international Christian charity working with churches in more than 130 countries providing resources to bring the good news about Jesus Christ to children, young people and families – and to encourage them to develop spiritually through the Bible and prayer. As well as our network of volunteers, staff and associates who run holidays, church-based events and school Christian groups, we produce a wide range of publications and support those who use our resources through training programmes.

How to use this book

 These daily notes are intended to help you to worship and to pray. Each day there is a short reading from the Bible, some thoughts and a prayer.

 The readings are from the *Easy-to-Read Version* (ETRV), a very clear and simple translation of the Bible. The reading printed each day is quite short. A longer reading is also given if you would like to read more using your own Bible.

The Bible, which is sometimes called the Word of God, is not really one book but a whole library of many books. The 66 books were written by many people that God spoke to at different times. At the front of the Bible you will find a list of the titles of all the books in the Bible and the page number where each book begins.

To help you find your way around such a big book, little groups of one or two sentences have been numbered, and then groups of those sentences have been collected into chapters.

So how do you find the one or two sentences that you want in the Bible? Let's say you want to find Matthew 5:5,6. That means you need to look in the book called Matthew, in chapter number 5 and verses 5 and 6.

You can find Matthew in the lists of books at the front of the Bible. In the *Easy-to-Read Bible*, Matthew starts on page 1109. So when you have turned to the beginning of Matthew you then search for chapter 5, which is on page 1113. Look down the page until you see the numbers 5 and 6. Those are the sentences (or verses) that you need.

When you do your Bible reading, try to spend a few extra minutes praying and worshipping. Prayer is talking and listening to God. You can do this aloud or without using words. You can pray on your own or with friends. Worship is telling God how much you love him, through words or songs, or things you do. This can be singing in church, but it's a lot more than that, too. It's about enjoying the wonderful world God has made. It's about how we speak to each other. It's about how we live our lives.

As you pray you can:

 thank God for his goodness and his help;

 tell God how great he is, and that you love him;

 ask God to help you, your friends, your family and other people.

If you are a helper using this book with someone who does not read, you will find guidance notes at the end.

The *Easy-to-Read Version* of the Bible is available to buy from Causeway PROSPECTS.

God gives new life

1   In the beginning

He [Jesus] was there with God in the beginning. All things were made through him. Nothing was made without him.
John 1:2,3 (Full reading John 1:1–4)

Jesus is very special. He has always been with his Father God. God and Jesus made the world together. They made the stars and the sun and the moon. They made the trees and the grass and the flowers. They made all the animals and all the people.

Look around you. See all the things that make you happy. Jesus and his Father God made them all.

Lord Jesus, thank you for giving us the sun and the moon and the stars. Thank you for the trees and the flowers. Thank you for the rain which makes the trees and flowers grow. Thank you for the birds and animals and fish. Thank you for my family and my friends. Amen.

2   God is good

Everything good comes from God. And every perfect gift is from God. These good gifts come down from the Father who made all the lights in the sky (sun, moon, stars). But God never changes like those lights. He is always the same.
James 1:17 (Full reading James 1:16–18)

God keeps his promises. God does not change. God is always the same. And everything that is good comes from God.

It's good to know God. God doesn't have bad moods or change his mind or break his promises. He is good all the time. God made the sun and the moon and the stars for us. God gives us good things because he loves us.

Father God, thank you that you are always the same. Thank you for the good things you give me. Whenever I have something to enjoy, help me to thank you. Amen.

3   God gives life

... this is eternal life: that people can know you, the only true God, and that people can know Jesus Christ, the One you sent.
John 17:3 (Full reading John 17:1–5)

We know that everything good comes from God. We know God made us. He gives us life. God made us to have a very special kind of life called eternal life or life that goes on forever.

This special life means God can be our father in heaven. God's son Jesus can be our friend. It means we can be part of God's family forever and ever.

God sent Jesus to show us what this special life is like and to show us God's love.

Father God, thank you for sending Jesus and for making me part of your family forever. Help me to understand more about this special life you want me to have. Amen.

4   Jesus understands us

 The Word [Jesus] became a man and lived among us.
John 1:14 (Full reading John 1:14–16)

 God sent Jesus to be born as a baby and to grow up in our world. Because Jesus is exactly like his Father God we can see how wonderful God is. Jesus is kind and good.

Jesus had brothers and sisters so he knew what it was like to live in a family. He was a carpenter, making things out of wood like chairs and doors. Can you think of some other things he might have made?

Jesus had many friends. But he also knew people who didn't like him and were mean to him. Jesus knows what it is like for us. God sent Jesus to be a friend for us.

 Father God, thank you for sending your own special Son to live with people like me. Thank you that Jesus knows what I feel like. Thank you that Jesus can be a friend to me. Amen.

5   Jesus can do anything

Jesus said to the servants, 'Fill those waterpots with water'. So the servants filled the pots to the top ... Then the man in charge of the wedding feast tasted it, but the water had become wine.
John 2:7,9 (Full reading John 2:1–11)

Jesus and his family were guests at a wedding and there was not enough wine to drink. This could have really spoiled the wedding party. So Jesus turned some water into wine.

Jesus could do this because he is God's Son. Jesus can do anything. He did this amazing thing to show people who he was so that they would listen to him. But he also did it just to help his friends!

And it wasn't ordinary wine he made. It was the very best wine. Jesus always does everything in the best way.

Father God, please help me to do things in the best way like Jesus does. Amen.

6 God knows our needs

Jesus said, 'Bring the bread and the fish to me'. Jesus took the five loaves of bread and the two fish. Jesus looked into the sky and thanked God for the food. Then Jesus divided the loaves of bread... All the people ate and were filled.
Matthew 14:18–20 (Full reading Matthew 14:13–21)

More than 5000 (five thousand) people followed Jesus to listen to him. The people had no food to eat and there was nowhere to buy any. All Jesus had was five loaves and two fish. But Jesus prayed to his Father God and God changed everything. There was enough food for all the people and even lots left over.

Jesus loved the people and showed his love for them by giving them food to eat. God will always give people what they really need. God will give you what you need too.

Father God, thank you for Jesus and the wonderful things he can do. Thank you that you know my needs and will give me what I need. Amen.

7   Jesus is the Good Shepherd

'I am the good shepherd. The good shepherd gives his life for the sheep.'
John 10:11 (Full reading John 10:11–15)

Everyone knew about sheep and shepherds in the days of Jesus. Shepherds looked after their sheep. They fed them and cared for them. The shepherds knew every sheep in their flock by name. If one was missing they would go and look until they found it!

Jesus was telling his friends that they were like the sheep and he was like the shepherd. Jesus would care for his friends and they would stay with him. One day Jesus would be killed caring for his friends so that we can all become part of God's family. That's what we mean when we say Jesus died to save us.

Thank you Lord Jesus for being my shepherd and caring for me. Thank you for loving me that much. Amen.

8   Jesus died for us

Christ [Jesus] himself died for you. And that one death paid for your sins. He was not guilty, but he died for people who are guilty. He did this to bring you all to God.
1 Peter 3:18 (Full reading 1 Peter 3:18)

Jesus always did what his Father God wanted him to do. But the rest of us sometimes think bad thoughts and say bad things which hurt people. Sometimes we do bad things as well. All these things are called sins.

Jesus was killed by bad men. They told lies about him and had him nailed to a cross until he died in terrible pain. Jesus did nothing wrong. But when he died he was being punished for all the bad things everyone else has done. And that means all the bad things we've done too.

If we say sorry to God and ask him to forgive us, he will. Jesus has already taken the blame for us.

Lord Jesus, thank you for loving me so much. I am sorry for the things I have done that hurt you. Please forgive me. Amen.

Some people did accept him [Jesus]. They believed in him. He gave something to those people who believed. He gave them the right to become children of God.
John 1:12 (Full reading John 1:10–13)

Some people would like to become part of God's special family but they think God will never love them because of the bad things they've done.

Is that what you think? Well, God does love you. Jesus has already taken the blame for the bad things. All you have to do is believe in Jesus and ask God to forgive you. Say sorry to God and he will not punish you.

God wants all kinds of people in his family. He wants rich people in his family. He wants poor people. He wants clever people and not so clever people. God wants everyone in his family.

Lord Jesus, I know that sometimes I think bad things and say bad things and do bad things. I am sorry. Please forgive me. Please help me to do what is right. Amen.

10   A helper forever

I will ask the Father, and he will give you another Helper [the Holy Spirit]. He will give you this Helper to be with you forever.
John 14:16 (Full reading John 14:15–17)

Last time we read how if we ask God to forgive us for the wrong things we have done then God will forgive us. He has promised. Then he will help us to do good things instead of bad things. He will send us a helper. The helper is called the Holy Spirit.

The Holy Spirit is God at work in our world. He doesn't have a body like us so he isn't just in one place. He can be everywhere, with everyone who belongs to God's family. If you have asked to be forgiven and to belong to God's family then the Holy Spirit is with you, now. You can't see him but he's there. Isn't that wonderful? And he will help you to do the things God wants.

Father God, thank you for sending the Holy Spirit to help me love you and please you by doing what you want. Amen.

11 God helps us to grow

'I am the vine and you are the branches. If a person continues in me and I continue in that person, then that person will make much fruit. But without me that person can do nothing.'
John 15:5 (Full reading John 15:1–5)

Vines are plants, a bit like small trees. Branches grow on the stems and grapes grow on the branches. The stems feed the branches and the branches feed the grapes so they will grow.

If we stay close to Jesus and listen to what he says then he will give us the things we need to grow stronger in our faith. He will give us more love for God. He will help us to understand the Bible better. He will send his Holy Spirit to help us.

Lord Jesus, thank you for the kind of feeding you give me that helps me grow stronger in believing and trusting you. Help me to stay close to you and learn from you. Amen.

12 Comfort when we are sad

 'What great blessings there are for the people that are sad now! God will comfort them.'
Matthew 5:4 (Full reading Matthew 5:1–12)

 Sometimes we are sad. Perhaps we are sad because we are sick or hurting or a friend has died or moved away. Perhaps we're sad because we're sorry about something we've done. If we talk to God about how we feel he promises to comfort us. That means he will make us feel much better. We will be blessed (happy) when God comforts us. We will see how much he loves us.

Is there something that you are sad or upset about at the moment? Or perhaps one of your friends or family is feeling sad about something? Talk to God about it and ask him to help.

 Dear Father God, thank you for promising to comfort me when I feel sad. And thank you especially for the love and happiness you give me. Amen.

13 Needing God's help

'What great blessings there are for the people that are humble! They will have the land God promised.'
Matthew 5:5 (Full reading Matthew 5:1–12)

Being humble means knowing that you need help, that you can't do everything by yourself. Jesus was humble. He knew he needed God to help him. Some people think they can get on OK without God. People who are humble know they need God to help them.

Jesus promises that people who are humble will 'have the land God promised'. This means they will live with God for ever. Think what that will be like! God will be able to help us all the time! When we know that, it makes us very blessed (happy).

Father God, help me to be humble and know how much I need you. Help me to do the things you want. Thank you for your promises to me. Amen.

14 Doing right

'What great blessings there are for the people that want to do right more than anything else. God will fully satisfy them.'
Matthew 5:6 (Full reading Matthew 5:1–12)

There are many times when you have to choose what to do. Do you watch TV or do you help with the washing up? Do you speak nicely to someone who has annoyed you or do you shout at them? Do you thank God every day or do you take no notice of him?

Jesus says that if we really want to do the right thing, God will satisfy us. It will be like when we have a lovely meal and have really enjoyed it. We will be satisfied because God will be pleased with what we have done. He will repay us by making us blessed (happy).

Father God, more than anything else I want to do the right things each day, things that please you. Help me to know which things are right and good and help me to do them. Amen.

15 Good thoughts (1)

'What great blessings there are for the people that are pure in their thinking! They will be with God.'
Matthew 5:8 (Full reading Matthew 5:1–12)

Pure means clean and good. God wants us to think about good things and have good thoughts. God is pleased when we think good thoughts. Wrong thoughts make us hurt other people. That hurts God too.

God's thoughts are always pure. We can ask God to help us to think about him and how good he is. Then it will be easier for us to think like he does.

Father God, please help me to think only about good things. Please help me to know what is right and to stop myself thinking about things you don't like. Amen.

16 Good thoughts (2)

Think about the things that are true and honourable and right and pure and beautiful and respected.
Philippians 4:8 (Full reading Philippians 4:8,9)

The Bible tells us to think good thoughts not bad ones. So how do we do that? It is sometimes hard to do.

What if someone has been horrible to you? You might start thinking, 'I hate that person. I wish they were dead'. Tell yourself, 'Stop!' Instead, think of something good about that person and thank God for him or her.

What if you find yourself thinking about something bad or something you shouldn't – maybe something nasty on TV? Tell yourself, 'Stop!' Instead think about Jesus, perfect and pure, and thank God for him.

Father God, when my thoughts are bad, help me to say 'Stop!' and change my thoughts to good ones. Amen.

17 Being a peace-maker

'What great blessings there are for the people that work to bring peace! God will call them his sons and daughters.'
Matthew 5:9 (Full reading Matthew 5:1–12)

Jesus came to teach people how to live in peace with one another. He is sad when we fight and quarrel.

God is especially pleased with people who bring peace. There are some special peace-makers whose job is to go to other countries to help people talk to each other. These peace-makers help important people become friends again.

But you can be a peace-maker too. Peace-makers are also ordinary people who say something kind or helpful to calm down someone else who is angry or hurt.

Father God, please help me to know what to do when people around me are angry with one another. Help me to think of something kind or helpful to say to make things better. Amen.

18   Being treated badly

'What great blessings there are for the people that are treated badly for doing good! The kingdom of heaven belongs to them.'
Matthew 5:10 (Full reading Matthew 5:1–12)

When we are doing what God wants we are letting God be in charge of our lives. That's what 'the kingdom of heaven' is all about.

Sometimes we will be treated badly for doing what God wants. People may laugh at us or call us names. That's what happened to Jesus.

But God loves people who go on doing good even if they are treated badly for doing it.

Father God, please help me always do what you want even when people are unkind to me because of it. Please help me to know how pleased you are when I do the things you want. Amen.

19 Making life better

'The kingdom of heaven is like yeast that a woman mixes into a big bowl of flour to make bread. The yeast makes all the dough (bread) rise.'

Matthew 13:33 (Full reading Matthew 13:31–33)

Yeast is one of the things you need to make bread. Bread with no yeast is flat and hard. Just a little bit of yeast is all you need to make bread much nicer – light and good tasting.

The kingdom of heaven is what happens when Jesus works in us. He wants us to be like the yeast in the bread. He wants us to make life nicer for other people.

What little things can you do to make life nicer for people? Maybe a smile or a word or a hug or doing something to help. Just like yeast makes bread better the things we do for other people will make their lives better.

Jesus, please show me what little things I can do that will make a big difference to other people. Amen.

20 Strong like rock

'Every person that comes to me and listens to my teachings and obeys ... is like a man building a house. He digs deep and builds his house on rock.'
Luke 6:47,48 (Full reading Luke 6:47–49)

Lots of people worry about life. They worry about money, about the future, about knowing what to do. Jesus was telling the people to listen to what he said and to do the right things. Then they would not worry.

The things Jesus said are written in the Bible. The Bible will tell us the right things to do. The Bible has answers to questions about life and money. Reading the Bible helps us to understand Jesus better and to know his promises. Jesus and his words will never change. They are like strong rock. We can trust in Jesus. We can trust in his Word (the Bible).

Lord Jesus, help me to do what the Bible says even when it's hard to do it. Thank you that you are strong like a rock and that I can believe in you and not worry about things. Amen.

21 A friend in need

'I tell you, maybe friendship is not enough to make him [your friend] get up to give you the bread. But he will surely get up to give you what you need if you continue to ask.'
Luke 11:8 (Full reading Luke 11:1–9)

Jesus tells the story of a man whose friend came to visit him very late at night. The man didn't have any food to give his friend so he asked another friend, one of his neighbours, for help. And his neighbour did help.

Jesus is our best friend. We can always ask him to help us or our friends, whatever sort of help we need. And we can be sure that Jesus will hear our prayer and he will help.

Do you have a friend who is in trouble? Say his or her name now, and ask Jesus to help.

Lord Jesus, you know all my friends and their needs. Please help them. Amen.

22 Keep on praying

'So I tell you, continue to ask, and God will give to you.'
Luke 11:9 (Full reading Luke 11:1–9)

In the last story we read about the man getting some bread from his neighbour for his visitor. The neighbour had gone to bed so he couldn't help straightaway. The man had to wait.

God always hears our prayers, but sometimes we have to wait. Jesus tells us to keep on asking and not give up. God will give us what we need.

Are there things you've prayed about? Are you still waiting for God to answer? You can be sure that God will answer when he knows it's the right time.

Father God, thank you for hearing my prayers. Teach me to keep on asking until I get an answer to my prayers. Amen.

23 Living to please God

A man had two sons. The younger son said to his father, 'Give me my part of all the things we own!' So the father divided the wealth with his two sons. Then the younger son gathered up all that he had and left. He travelled far away to another country. There the son wasted his money living like a fool ... The son was so hungry that he wanted to eat the food that the pigs were eating. But no person gave him anything.'
Luke 15:11–13,16 (Full reading Luke 15:11–20)

Jesus told this story about a son who wasted all his money. He spent all his money on useless things. When it was all gone he could not buy food and no one would help him.

God loves us and gives us what we need but sometimes we do things we shouldn't! We waste what God has given to us. This makes God sad. It can make us very sad too.

Lord Jesus, please teach me to be careful about how I live. Show me what to do to please you. Amen.

The boy realised that he had been very foolish. He thought, 'All of my father's servants have plenty of food. But I am here, almost dead because I have nothing to eat. I will leave and go to my father. I will say to him: 'Father, I sinned against God and have done wrong to you.'
Luke 15:17,18 (Full reading Luke 15:11–20)

The son knew that he had been foolish and went home to say sorry to his father. When we do things wrong we can always go to God who is our Father and tell him we are sorry. Then he will forgive us.

When we say sorry to God about something, he promises not to remember that thing again.

When we do wrong things we make God sad as well as hurting other people. The son in the story realised this. Have you done wrong things? Do you want to say sorry to God?

Father God, I am sorry about ... (say what you have done wrong). Please forgive me. Amen.

25 Forgiving (1)

While the son was still a long way off, his father saw him coming. The father felt sorry for his son. So the father ran to him. He hugged and kissed his son. The son said, 'Father, I sinned against God and have done wrong to you. I am not good enough to be called your son'. But the father said to his servants, 'Hurry! Bring the best clothes and dress him ... '
Luke 15:20–22 (Full reading Luke 15:20–24)

The father loved his son and was waiting for him to come home. The father ran to welcome his son as soon as he saw him. The son hardly had time to say he was sorry. The father was ready to forgive his son because he loved him so much.

God is ready to forgive us just like that. And God wants us to show love to other people by forgiving them when they do or say things to hurt us.

Father God, thank you that you are always ready to forgive us! Help me to show others your love by forgiving people even when they hurt me. Amen.

The older son was angry and would not go in to the party ... The son said to his father, 'I have served you like a slave for many years! ... you never gave a party for me and my friends. But your other son has wasted all your money ... Then he comes home, and you kill the fat calf for him!'
Luke 15:28–30 (Full reading Luke 15:25–32)

This is the next part of the story about the son who wasted all his money. When he got home his brother was jealous. He thought his father loved his younger brother more. He didn't realise that his father loved both his sons. So the older son was angry with his father.

The father wasn't angry. He forgave. Is there someone who has hurt you? Forgive that person now and God will take away the pain of what that person did. Remember only the good things about the person. Try to forget about what they did.

Father God, I forgive ... (say the person's name) for what they did. Amen.

27 Forgiving (3)

'You must truly forgive your brother and sister, or my heavenly Father will not forgive you.'
Matthew 18:35 (Full reading Matthew 18:23–35)

Jesus told another story, this time about a king. The king's servant owed him a lot of money. The servant asked for time to pay it back. The king agreed. Then the servant went to a friend who owed him a small amount of money. The friend also asked for time to pay. But the servant refused and had him thrown into prison. When the king found out, he was very angry.

God has forgiven all of us for lots of wrong things we have done. We might have done things that upset someone. We might have said something that has hurt a friend. God has forgiven us and he wants us to forgive other people. He will not be happy with us if we don't forgive other people.

Father God, thank you so much for forgiving me! You are so loving to me. Please help me forgive other people for whatever they have done to me. Amen.

28　Showing God's love

'I give you a new command: Love each other. You must love each other like I loved you. All people will know that you are my followers if you love each other.'
John 13:34,35 (Full reading John 13:34,35)

In this book we have been finding out about God's goodness and his love. We have been learning how to live in a way that pleases God.

Today's verse says we must show God's love to other people.

How can we do that? How can we help people to see how much God loves them?

Here is something you could try. Start every day by praying that God will help you see how good he is and how much he loves people. Then when you meet people you will be able to tell them 'God is good' or 'He loves you'.

Father God, please fill me with your love so I can help other people to know your goodness and your love. Amen.

'He decided how much each servant would be able to care for. The man gave one servant five bags of money. He gave another servant two bags of money. And he gave a third servant one bag of money.'
Matthew 25:15 (Full reading Matthew 25:14–30)

In this story a man gave his servants a lot of money to look after for him. Some of the servants used what they had been given to make even more money for the man. The man was pleased with those servants and rewarded them.

Jesus has given each of us something special that we can do so that other people can know about him. You might be able to sing, pray for a friend, tidy up, or help look after someone. Jesus is pleased when we do things like this.

Jesus, please show me how I can use the special things you've given me – my gifts – to help others to know you. Amen.

30 A party in heaven!

'... the angels of God are very happy when one sinner changes his heart.'
Luke 15:10 (Full reading Luke 15:8–10)

This story in the Bible is about a woman who lost a silver coin. She looked everywhere for it. When she found the lost coin, she wanted everyone to be happy with her.

Some people don't know that God cares for them. They take no notice of him!

Whenever someone finds out that God loves them and they stop taking no notice of God, all God's angels celebrate. The angels have a party in heaven because that person has come to God.

Father God, thank you so much that there is a party in heaven whenever someone believes in God and starts living a new life following Jesus. I pray that my friend will soon get to know you and find out about your love. Help me to know what to say and what to do to help. Amen.

Key words

Amen   We usually say this at the end of prayers and it means, 'That's my prayer too'.

Bless   To show kindness to someone. To do them a good turn.

Cross   To be cross is to be angry, bad-tempered.

Cross   A cross is two big pieces of wood in the shape of a cross. Jesus was nailed to a cross when he was killed.

Foolish   Silly.

Forgive   When you forgive someone who has hurt you, you're not cross with them anymore.

Holy Spirit   The Holy Spirit is a person. He is the third person of the Trinity with Father God and Jesus, his Son. The Holy Spirit is God at work on the earth.

Judgement   Deciding what is right and what is wrong.

Lord   The one in charge. Another word for God.

Peace   Quiet, calm, not worrying.

Powerful   Strong.

Praise	To tell God (or a person) how good they are.
Pray	Talk to God or Jesus about things.
Psalm	A song written to God.
Punishment	What happens to a person who is caught doing something bad or wrong.
Rule	To rule is to be in charge.
Save	To rescue, set free, or keep safe.
Sin / Sins	Bad things people do that make God sad and hurt other people.
Worship	Telling God how much you love him through words or songs or things you do.

Notes for carers and helpers

These Bible notes are designed to help a wide a range of people who need extra help. It's impossible to tailor Bible notes to fit everyone's needs. But our hope is that many who have some level of visual or intellectual disability or just need a simpler approach can be helped to pray and read the Bible regularly through this series.

Some people will be able to use these notes without any help from others. But if you are the carer or helper of someone needing some assistance with using them, here are a few pointers which may be useful to you.

Before you begin, ask the Holy Spirit to help communicate the main thought from each reading and note to the person you are reading with. God through the Holy Spirit can communicate on levels that we cannot! Part of the Holy Spirit's role is to make Jesus real to people and you are working in partnership with him.

Make sure you have the person's full attention before starting to read. Think about how you can eliminate auditory or visual distractions in the environment such as TV or other people. Try to find a quiet place. Use eye contact to maintain good connection.

Read slowly and clearly, pausing where suitable. Facial expressions, hand and body movements can all help to underline the meaning of the material. Encourage whatever response is appropriate, particularly in prayer and praise.

Use your knowledge of the person to assess how much is being understood, how much clarification might be needed and how to best make applications more relevant.

Make your time together an opportunity for learning and fellowship for both of you.

Other titles in the Bible Prospects series:

Being like Jesus

Songs of praise

The story of Christmas

Scripture Union produces a wide range of Bible reading notes for people of all ages and Bible-based material for small groups.   SU publications are available from any Christian bookshop.   For information and to request free samples and a free catalogue of Bible resources:

- phone SU's mail order line: local rate number 08450 706 006

- email info@scriptureunion.org.uk

- fax 01908 856020

- log on to www.scriptureunion.org.uk

- write to SU Mail Order, PO Box 5148, Milton Keynes MLO, MK2 2YX